A COWTOWN CHRONICLE

WILLIAM D. BARNEY
POETRY

Margee West

In appreciation for
your beautiful design!

William D Barney

Photo: Norm Tindell, *Fort Worth Star-Telegram*

A COWTOWN CHRONICLE

WILLIAM D. BARNEY
POETRY

BB

BROWDER SPRINGS BOOKS
DALLAS, TEXAS

Other books by William D. Barney

Kneel From the Stone
Permitted Proof
A Little Kiss of the Nettle
The Kildeer Crying
Long Gone to Texas
A Reach of Wilderness
In a State of Euphorbia
Words from a Wide Land

~

Copyright 1999 © Browder Springs Books and William D. Barney
Cover Photographs: Copyright © Arthur Meyerson 1999
Edited by Betsy Colquitt

Library of Congress Catalog card number 99-63241

ISBN 0-9651359-3-4 (alk. paper)

This book is the third of the American Regional Book Series
from Browder Springs.

Printed in the United States of America
Design/ Margie Adkins Graphic Design

Contents

The Town

A Man of Letters

When William Barney calls himself as "a man of letters," he stakes this claim on his thirty-five years as a U.S. Postal Service employee, not on his other and longer career as poet. This latter career began when as a student in Central (now Paschal) High in Fort Worth, he discovered that he liked poetry and enjoyed writing it. As *A Cowtown Chronicle* confirms, his talent as poet is alive and well after six decades. His poems have appeared in many journals and since 1952, in eight of his poetry collections, which have earned him both regional and national awards. Of his many recognitions, perhaps the most notable came in 1982 when he received The Robert Frost Memorial Award, funded by Holt, Rinehart and Winston and offered through the Poetry Society of America.

Now in his eighties, Barney still practices the craft he describes as "one of the great joys of life a person can stumble into." But in fact, his poems don't "stumble" nor did he "stumble" into being a poet. He's carefully studied many poets, among them, Frost, W.B.Yeats, and Wallace Stevens. Like the poets he admires, Barney is a careful craftsman whose well-made poems are accessible and inviting even to readers who usually shun poetry as too hard and demanding to be pleasant reading.

Poems in *A Cowtown Chronicle* show Fort Worth's past and present, its flora and fauna, and some of its many and varied people, and thus reveals much that defines this place and affects those who live here. Such showing helps "to make us see," which the novelist Joseph Conrad praised as literature's major achievement. Barney proves an excellent mentor to those of us who know the city, and to those less familiar with this locus, his poems provide a gracious introduction.

A Cowtown Chronicle draws on the city's heritage as a livestock market which led to the North Side meat industry and the Stockyards complex, built, as he writes, "of mortar and red meat." And there's the Trinity, a sometimes puny river that until tamed by dams and lakes could be dangerous but has always been essential to the city. Where the Trinity flows near the Belknap Bridge, there are birds, important denizens of Barney's city and his larger world, and here and elsewhere, there are plants, especially native ones few of us can name, but he knows their names—both popular and scientific—and passes these and their lore along to us. A longtime resident of Riverside, he knows his neighborhood, and like Henry David Thoreau in Concord, has "traveled much" in it. He knows that come fall, his walks will take him to the pecan trees by the river, where he'll fill his pockets with so many nuts that his trip home will leave a telltale pecan trail.

He often reminds us too of how the past enters the present as in "Lady with the Calliope." In an annual downtown Stock Show Parade, the Lady playing her steam-powered keyboard becomes the symbol of the parade's many musicians making their many kinds of music. The poem suggests too the wonder of the art of music and its sister art of poetry. In Greek myth, Calliope is the muse of epic poetry, Euterpe the muse of music. Past and present also meld in a visit to Log Cabin Village, where the poet-viewer marvels at a perfectly fashioned water wheel that once turned wheat into flour, and wonders on the unknown craftsman who joined the pieces of wood to shape the durable wheel.

Another kind of hero from the past is Bill Pickett, whose skill in riding and wrestling bulls created a still-unchallenged cowboy legend.

Other poems in the collection focus on the contemporary city in which arts other than those of the cowboy flourish. In "At the Van Cliburn" and other poems on music—a lifelong interest of Barney—treats of music different from that of the Stock Show Parade. So too does "My Watts and the Whirlwind," in which Andre Watts continues his piano recital at TCU as our most recent tornado touches down on the campus. Barney finds subjects in museums other than Log Cabin Village, as in "Showdown at the Amon Carter." The museum's Frederic Remington and Charles Russell collections evoke the painters' contrasting visions of the American West and their mutual recognition that works they created belonged to a remembered and much loved West that was sadly changed by the time they were doing their paintings and sculptures.

Fort Worth's present is the focus in many other poems, including "A Modern Stonehenge," which notes the kinship between the city's skyline of towering structures and the stone-age monument on Salisbury Plain. Similarly, the poet sees the flight patterns of Carswell NAS planes over the city as suggesting the inevitable joining of large and small worlds, and of the distant and the near.

Though diverse in its subjects and themes, *A Cowtown Chronicle* remains reader-friendly, even when the poet's interpretations of our mutual place surprise us by seeing the familiar in new ways. Always too, Barney's style is engaging even when poetic forms he uses are demanding. He handles with equal ease the "open verse" form of most poems here. Notable too in the collection is the poet's good spirit and love for that he writes of.

A resident of Fort Worth since 1928, William Barney knows this part of space in which he's spent most of his life. For a city celebrating its 150th birthday, *A Cowtown Chronicle* is a gift to enjoy and cherish. It's likely too that those who celebrate later Fort Worth birthdays will benefit by discovering William Barney's vision of the place he knows by heart and lets others of us know through his poems.

Betsy Colquitt

At Home in the World

The title, *A Cowtown Chronicle*, limits the scope of William Barney's newest work. Colleagues and friends suggested the title was not poetic enough, too plain and certainly limited. Poets, as do other writers, strive for the universal even in the specific, and titles often seem deliberately mysterious, inviting the reader to find out why a volume was so named. Barney is a master of such titles—*In a State of Euphorbia, A Little Kiss of the Nettle, The Killdeer Crying*, to name a few. However, 1999 marks the Sesquicentennial of Fort Worth, Texas, and the poet saw no reason to beat around the bush with the title since each piece is in one way or another a declaration of his admiration for and devotion to "The queen city of the prairies," another early label for Fort Worth.

If the poet writes himself, title and all, right into a corner, he also writes himself right out of it. In Barney's hands, Cowtown becomes the universal *place* and readers who have their own notions of place know exactly whereof and "what of" he speaks whether they live on another continent or speak another language. He's writing about home and the territory that sustains it, giving it shape and meaning.

If the poet's subject is limited, it is never restricted, confined, or hemmed in; never square. The presence of the Trinity River sees to that and the poet uses the waterway to define the fluid boundaries of his kingdom.

Riverside, the east side, is the area in which Barney lives and has lived almost all his life. It is where Lori, the girl, swings and his family listened while sitting at the kitchen table, to *Lenore* with "spoons in mid-air." The best neighbor is Mount Olivet Cemetery where "in the encampment for the dead/the downed leaves will not be still" and where, at the appointed time, Barney will become "a kinsman to both leaf and wind, to the stir among things of earth."

On the upper west side of the river is Northside, known know as the Historic Stockyards District, which measured the early days in pens, ramps, hooves; where "on the banks of Marine Creek/Pickett bulldogged with a will."

The fort-town-city sits in the fork of the Trinity. Bridges and streets yearn river-ward. Traffic flows—"currents of change circle about" near the bluff "where the troopers camped,/where (they say) lean men on horseback/drove their herds down to the river."

Bridges span but also provide sanctuary for whatever gathers by the water—gnats, mosquitoes, cliff swallows which

> regain their place
>
> in the groins of the bridge
> reconnoitering, mating, constructing
> founding once more the shape of home.

A bullsnake under the Belknap bridge rejects the presence of humans:

> If only he'd had hands
> to have thumbed his nose—the way he slowly
> withdrew.

The poet recalls the funeral of Commodore Basil Muse Hatfield who once kept a scow under a bridge and whose ashes were discovered some forty-five years after and scattered from the same bridge, the ashes

> of a man who made his way by scow
> down the Trinity River,
> the Coastal Canal,
> all the way up the Mississippi
> on to the Chicago World's fair.

The courthouse has the best view of the Trinity where "that imposing pile/of freckled granite, bare to the sun,/has lifted a dome on the high bluff/where the founders camped."

Beard-tongues, ginkoes, saw-toothed daisies, pecan trees in Riverside Park, grass, leaves, decorate, line, beckon the reader to river's side to smell, touch, hear.

In the next-to-last poem of the collection, Barney hangs Fort Worth in "that horseshoe bend of river" like "a golden cage" bathed in last rays of a late afternoon in December where "Men coming from the East may see it glow."

Important as the Trinity is, the link is never overstated. And, if the Trinity grounds the volume, then music informs it. Barney is a musician, and his knowledge, love, and understanding of musical forms are descant to the theme of place. Some poems are specifically about music. He tells in a note to a poem about sheep that it "may almost be sung to the tune of Bach's 'Sheep May Safely Graze.'" In another, he strives, along with other "solemn not very flexible basses" to sing Bach's Magnificat. He recalls Andre Watts' performance during a tornado, ponders a playing at the Van Cliburn which puts him in awe of "the chemistry". . . "that ties together finger and brain in instant prodigy" and thinks about the "holy howl" of bagpipes in church. His Christmas carol marvels that "to see if it be safe for us/ a King should taste of death." Included is an arrangement written by his son, Ronald, which has been performed often at First Presbyterian Church where Barney has been a member for many years.

Barney's use of words and language engage the reader. Many writers in whatever genre confess that words are not always their friends. Some try to grab, trap, cajole, force, manipulate. Barney, however, never shoves words around or runs after them carelessly. Instead, words seem to rush out joyfully to meet him. The poet invites us into a world made familiar with words.

Even the forms chosen by the poet enchant, pulling us in cunning ways, deeper into place. Rhyme, no rhyme, set forms, and patterns or combinations of several, inverting standard syntax, rhythms provided by an internal metronome ticking to the stuff of language—all fuse the reader to place.

Love of words brought me to the work of William Barney; that and an affinity for his subject matter. The poet takes me not into a strange place but into the well-known. Fort Worth is also my Beloved City. I have observed intimately every building, site, character, landscape, creature, atmosphere and attitude about which he writes. But I never absorbed any of it rightly until reading *A Cowtown Chronicle*; until I saw the metaphoric city from afar rising out of the prairie in a curve of the Trinity, its buildings outlined and illuminated in the fiery Texas sun, singing from then to now and forever.

Joyce Gibson Roach

4

THE POEMS

THE ARTS AND ARDORS

A Wine Vessel at the Kimbell

He looks at us out of buried centuries
with undimmed defiance; but it is not fear
disquiets us; rather we halt in awe
perceiving his formidable intricacies;
that rake of body, buttock to poll,
the pleated wedge of enormous neck,
solid stability of huge hooves—
rightness and deftness of the whole—
noble proportions, flawlessly wrought
not in bronze nor gold-and-silver inlay
but in the timeless metal of a mind
and hand, a fluid in infinity caught
so that we think: a Craftsman knew this bulk
snorting and tossing the sleek-horned snout,
galloping lightly on earth rattling feet;
saw and was ravished by the delicate bulk
and made him an image to perpetuate
the mighty loins, the grotesque, heavy head,
the thick agility, the great broad back—
ponderous perfection, chaste, elate.

In this green vessel there is poured such wine
as makes our flesh dream of antiquity
older even than Zhou or Quin, an age
when out of nothingness came sudden design;
when this we give the name *Rhinoceros,*
a stiffening concept in the churning flux,
gathered himself out of seething atoms
and boldly shed the primordial fosse.
Here, now, he stands, in every point exact,
embellished, belligerent, implausible brute
belief cannot deny nor memory
undo the grace of accomplished fact.

$\sim$

The Clydesdales

What do we need of behemoths, mastodons,
     dinosaurs,
to astonish the apertures of our reason,
seeing we have these sleek, gargantuan horses
swishing their silky feet, making musical clop
on our pavement? The great brown Clydesdales,
perfectly matched in team and in tandem,
faces ablaze and rattling their leather
     armor,
advance through our streets on enormous
     hooves;
nobler by far than a column of tanks,
they ponderously glide like a great steam
     monster
easily clanking into a station.
               They pass us by,
strutting like feathery-footed pigeons,
lifting each indefatigable bolt
and smashing it gently on asphalt horizons.
Down Houston they haughtily drag their wagon—
these who knew knighthood when Man was in
     flower,
up Main and back to the granite-skinned
     courthouse,
a foam, a fine lather ashine on their flanks.
Beautiful beasts, how did you ever find grace
     to submit
in your terrible dominance, in your cyclotron
     stride,
to the bit to the bridle, to harness and
     swingletree
and the puny five-fingered hand, the cunning
     reinmaster?

The Lady and the Calliope

The lady playing the Calliope
coming up Main Street in the Parade—
how can she hear what the music is saying
here on the yellowing pavement?
The scream of the steam pipes
overpowers: she is trapped in the roar
between buildings, how can she guess how it goes
except by her fingers? The soft clunk of hooves,
the smacking of cymbals, the intermittent drums,
a swarm of children blowing blue horns,
those whoops of possemen stirring themselves—
she sits in her cloud of steam oblivious
and the patient draft animals that pull
her fiendish chariot of fume, they know nothing
of triumph; they plod obediently.
They too do not know the music.

All of us crowded on the curbs, in second-storys,
up in the steelwork of the new skyscrapers,
we only dimly guess the name of the tune.
It is History. A noise that is always sounding,
always too loud to be gathered at once
with a comfortable ear. Now, while it happens,
who recognizes which theme is which,
one motif from another? How can we comprehend
what the music is saying
when there's a Calliope passing by?

~

A Sheep is Safely Grazed

Here on a rack she is poised, immobile,
head in a trap while her body's ravished,
  this gentle Suffolk ewe is
   forced to give up her wrinkled
fleece, in plain sight of all who pass
through the low stalls in the sheep barn.

This is not fair: it is cold and cruel
to be transfixed like a sculptor's model
  while her exhibitor shapes her,
   carefully clipping, carving—
look how it falls, the dingy wool,
off her fat sides and off her rounded rump.

  But even now, a deed made clear and pure
  brightens in our eyes, a cool, Carrara form.

See, how she stands now in perfect raiment,
back a white bank of pure snow, new-fallen,
  is she not chaste and blooming
   like a dull bud fresh-opened,
trimmed as a bride to tread the aisle
could she break free this raw restraint?

                      ~

(May almost be sung to the tune of
Bach's "Sheep May Safely Graze.")

In the Cattlebarn

Rows of stalls, oatstraw and dung
in the cattlebarn;
boys grooming the fat steers,
trimming their strawberry pelts,
fluffing out round curls,
gunning them down with black blow-driers.
Even the hooves must be filed and polished.
Presently in the arena,
competing to see which will make the best
        cuts,
sleek symphonies of roasts and sirloins,
they'll have to waddle.

Like sending washed children to school
or pushing them, older, into brutal war,
putting fresh bodies on the block
(the slaughter here is slower).

You can see how the hands fondling the hair
dread what is coming;
even in the moment of pride they tremble,
knowing that boys have to be men,
that steers, inevitably, make meat.

                  ~

Canticle for a Cutting Horse

Dun as an oak leaf dead, triggered and taut
    upon wind is the mare, the palomino.
She dances upon tanbark, a ballerina, a blade
    of exquisite balance;
her flesh is a furious woman,
a blend of desire and dissent, and of power
    and delicate motion;
chastely the saddle begirds her,
and the rider bestride bends like a whip
    as she pivots.

Relaxed in her sensitive step, patient yet
    wholly alert, the mare,
the palomino, walks the tight-rope of the
    lightning.
Shall I say she is merely animal, creature of
    instant, instinctive precision,
the flower of bestial blood?
She is spirtuelle, she aspires toward flame,
    to the fools' fire in dark pastures.
Her skin is a pumpkin smoke,
a smoldering satin, the dust of an evening
    cloud.

In her sleek strength the mare shall, as men,
    have glory,
but in her responsive heart let her rejoice.
    She is poised as a fencer's foil,
she stalks her prey like a tigress;
like a spider she weaves the kinetic web of
    enclosure,
she throws her great breast as a shuttle.

Make her a symbol for mind, a talisman
    in her tawniness
for any who praise pursuit
of the quick metaphor, the well-cinched
    word, the honest, honorable tone,
the summer within the seed.
Make her a ballad seeking right speech,
    a strophe kindling to song.

Yet none of these you make her.
She herself is sufficient, the palomino,
    the perfect, the slim-legged mare;
leave her to the high mesas,
to the rust-rimmed llano, her proper
    stage; let her dance
her tango of intricate measures.
Nothing shall match her image, nothing
    shall rightly encompass
her competence, her brute beauty.

~

The Slide

In the Children's Zoo, when it's Stock Show time,
there's a devilish contraption, the duckling slide.
It's a sort of a stair, with a pond below,
and not much else for ducklings to do.
We all gather round to watch them climb
up to the top of this treacherous trap,
where the bait hangs high for ducklings to grab.
It hangs out of reach, oh, maybe not quite.
Still, what hungry duckling won't give it a try?
When he misses, he's bound to lose footing
and down the slide go bewilderedly shooting.
We all of us gathered here shout with glee
to see a poor duckling cheated this way.

I have this fantasy, of somewhere above
a gaggle of Ultra-Ducks looks down on us
hilariously quacking at our over-reach
as we slide on our tails down into the deep.

If a man's reach must exceed his grasp,
it's only fair ducklings face the same fact.
Prizes get hung where they can't be snatched
(say some) whether ducklings or men get hatched.

~

Bill and Clown

The bull has no sense of humor;
he is not in a mood to be messed with
by one more two-legged tormentor.
He has disposed of the one who stayed
for almost a minute behind his hump;
now this clown who insolently thumbs nose,
who dodges adroitly, nimbly climbs a wall,
or hides in a barrel, engages his rage.

The bull does not take kindly to jests.
He snorts, his eyes bulge with fury.
His wicked horns rake the air.
He charges and misses, he charges again.
We all know one of these days
he will not miss. The savage verb gore
has a cousin noun, which will mottle
the tanbark; the clown will make faces
of searing pain.
              But this is the moment
we all have been waiting for, this duel
between bull and clown. Other events
caught our interest: man against steer,
bucking horses, proud riders,
smart ropers. This one, though
has sublimity. It is about
the funny clown and the ferocious bull,
about Man confronting Monster.
It is about danger and dexterity,
the skill of the quick-footed,
the gasp of thousands watching enthralled.

What this is about, most of all, is
terror, the almost promise of death.
                            ~

A Ballad for Bill Pickett

Willie got born somewhere near Austin,
    a Texan as all agree.
He was some Black and some Creole
    and part of him Cherokee.

He learned to ride before he could walk,
    leastways, that's as they say.
He'd stay in a saddle on a bucking bronc
    or out on the range all day.

He saw some cowboys branding calves;
    they couldn't catch the brutes.
Willie, he said, "I'll catch you a few,
    as sure as my feet is in boots."

They laughed at the skinny kid as he rode
    for a calf that was on the run;
he slid from his horse, grabbed the head,
    and down in the dirt they spun.

And the calf held taut. They still tell
    how Willie had got him a grip,
for he held on to that yearling's head
    with his teeth in its upper lip.

"I seen a bulldog do that once,"
    said Willie when he was through.
"I says to myself, if a dog can do that,
    no reason I can't too."

His fame went through the cities around,
    how he could take down a steer,
grabbing its head and chawing its lip—
    he was a man without fear.

He even went down to Mexico City
    to work a wild bull in the ring.
If the crowd hadn't tossed brickbats,
    he'd have bulldogged the damn thing.

The Miller Brothers of 101 Ranch
    got word of Willie's fame.
Zack Miller, he came down to Cowtown
    to see him play his game.

There on the banks of Marine Creek
    Pickett bulldogged with a will.
Said Zack, "Join us, you're our man,
    and your name is henceforth Bill."

They held a big fair near Guthrie Town,
    the biggest ever was seen
in the Territory, complete with horses,
    stagecoaches, a beauty queen,

Two hundred Indians from a dozen tribes,
    at their head Old Geronimo.
And cowboys by dozens and dignitaries—
    oh, it was a marvelous show!

But the biggest event of the whole day
    was bulldogging by our Bill.
He did himself proud, he showed them how
    and gave that crowd a true thrill.

He was with Millers the rest of his days,
    a showman they counted a friend.
When a wild horse kicked him in the head,
    Bill came to an untimely end.

And Old Zack Miller wrote a poem to say
    how "Old Bill is Dead" but still
would live on in the hearts of men.
    There'd never be any like Bill.

On Exchange Avenue, North Fort Worth,
    there's a sculpture of a brave man,
of a struggling steer got by the horns—
    it's all to an artful plan.

Friends, honor the cowboy. Bill Pickett.
    He was tough. He was good. He was game.
He fought with his hands, his heart, his teeth,
    and he won himself a proud name.

Rider and Sea

That lone rider in a tempest of horns,
a maelstrom of frightened steers—
all here, frozen in a sea of bronze
slashing an empty edge of North Main.
They seem aware, enormously alive,
yet all are caught in the clutch of time,
silent, unmoving, fixed pawns of history.
Wild longhorns, lashed into turbulence,
they twist lank flesh till it screams,
they flash great heads as if lightning
set fire to bone. They will not be turned
from their rush to freedom.

      How can the puny horseman,
mere cowboy, still that wild stampede?
How can he dare the forest of snags,
not be impaled? Surely some angry power
pitched him against these running beasts.
Malignant destiny tosses him here
into a storm of implacable forces.

A theme from an old chorus, a song
of triumph out of Handel,
that savage vaunt at Pharaoh's undoing,
teases my mind: "The Horse and his Rider!"
The words speak a curse for the cowboy,
caught in this terrible tide,
they taunt him, he cannot calm this fury:
or stay these fierce ones in flight:
"The Horse and his Rider"—a fierce cry
at the overthrow of mortal men:
"The Horse and his Rider
has He thrown into the sea!"

            ~

Science and History

These we have seen. These we remember:
the tusks of the mastodon;
the Samurai warrior; Babbage's wheels;
the saurian skeletons in their dance
of survival; the dome of immensity
where the helicopter lifts
dragging, almost, us out of our seats;
the Gentling mockingbird, singing in paint;
stooped cavemen trepanning a dull head;
Old William Jenkins Worth, his uniform,
saluting us out of our history;
a gathering of wolves; tin Lizzies.

Memory won't hold all the store.
How do we ever assimilate
the artifacts and the knowledge,
the passions of time and the arts?
They stir in the mind, they move about,
they settle into solitary spaces.
We never know for sure all they mean,
though we seek inward to remember.

A Balanced Wheel
The Log Cabin Village, Fort Worth

He'd never built a wheel before.
It took a lot of studying about
ever before he laid hand to wood.
A wheel for water. There was more
to a wheel than he understood
at the first or ever did find out.
How do you get the thing to balance?
That, he learned quick, was the
    principal nut.
To give it lines and shape it so
every point had its countervailance;
no part of the round, no blade or
    strut
turned catawampus under the flow.
No, if it rolled, it wouldn't lope,
else likely it lunged itself apart.
He had to shave off paper-thin,
first here, then there, and sweat
    and hope
the monster contained itself within
the clumsy circle of wooden art.
He had to see that every pound
of the fabrication kept on course—
didn't compete or go flying off
but bent obedient, transferred force
from the race of water in a trough
to the thick axle toiling round.
That's balance. With it, catch a drip
and make it grind a bushel of grain.
Set it notching a coiled spring
and time itself will march and trip.
Even, say some, fastened to a brain,
it can make sense out of anything.

Craftsman
Log Cabin Village, Fort Worth

Whose the hand which for its own purpose
notched tree trunks with skill and with patience
strong to stand through time so tight-cornered?
      Give him due honor.

See, where axe bit out the clean dovetail
squarely, holding in grooved precision:
till oak logs made union for
      longer than men do.

Ask then, why that painstaking ardor?
Ruder cabins, hewn roughly to order,
keep against weather and hard pillage
      a lifetime enough.

Wind might pull apart a dry shingle;
locked timbers hold an edge on tempests;
thieves, marauders, hardly break fitted
      wood in tough angles.

All these point to but one conclusion:
back of axe, of arm, was the purpose
which in time would fashion a lasting
      print of its presence.

Call it craftsmanship, for remembrance—
some foresightful hand joyed in setting
marks to linger where he smote, saying
      proudly, *I made it.*

A Magnificance of Melismas

Here in one room we all are sat,
six solemn not very flexible basses,
together attacking *The Magnificat*,
dutifully thumping the wily phrases,
spurred in the maze by a noble bassoon,
we toil to unravel the intricate tune.

Why did he make his melisma austere,
un-Handel-like, unpredictable,
joy in giving the wound inflictable
on stubborn tissue behind the ear?
I ask myself, but also old Bach
why he should shape his sacred score
so devilish-difficult? For such store,
why do we labor to pick the lock?

Ah-ah-ah-ah-ni-ma-may-ah!
(It says no more than, in English, 'My soul')
Sir, was your hand quite out of control
to set notes down like a mad bricklayer?
Meanwhile, the bassoon is setting our pace:
press the right keys and the pages purl.
But how do I wobble my larynx in bass
without getting lost in the glorious swirl?

Om-nes Om-nes gen-e-ra-ci-o-nes:
the churn of sound inexorably
imposes order, like a white furnace
seraphim-choired. We sing better than we
know how, the cry going up on high.
Numbness, numbness—yet we magnify:
particles in a storm, we fly.

He knew Mystery, that much is clear;
see in his confident weaving together,
spinning in gold from his masterful tether
a garment of praise for the Maiden's cheer.
Creation's an opus never done
(I hear him announce in recitative.)
Let the voice strive to fulfil the run,
the lung will learn stamina to believe.

⁓

Bagpipes in Church

The bagpipes hither skirling,
   how can we sing the hymn?
I cannot keep the measure,
   so do they twitch my limb.
The Old Hoot knows I am fit to stray
whenever the pipes begin to play.

I hear them squeal so fairly,
   now up, now down, and drone—
that shriek of strangled high note
   all who sing bass have known.
Lord, forgive us of the choir
who cannot reach where we aspire.

We sing our thanks for pipers
   with wit and will to sound:
and for that rough sea captain
   high mercy made abound.
For all who lift a grateful face
to the outpouring of true grace.

Was it not our Singing Master
   who taught us, Dance to the pipe?
Or gray, or bald, or downy,
   whosoever wears the stripe,
may fling aside his Sunday scowl
and join the bagpipes holy howl.

A Carol of the Gift of God

How can it be, the Force that gave
  both time and space their powers—
how can it stoop to bind itself,
  inhabit flesh like ours?

We who are dust motes in the sun,
  that He should magnify
us with His love, such shining truth
  I cannot reason why.

To see if it be safe for us
  a King should taste of death,
test the thin garment of our days
  by putting on our breath—

Come, Brothers, Sisters, sing for joy!
  The Gift of God made known
is wrapped in tissue and in trim
  as mortal as our own.

A Carol of the Gift of God

Words by William Barney • Music by Ron Barney

How can it be? the Force that gave both
Time and Space their powers, How can it stoop to
bind it - self, in - habit flesh like ours?

2. We who are dust motes in the sun, that He should magnify us with
His love, such shining Truth, I cannot reason why.
3. To see if it be safe for us, A King should taste of death, test the
thin garment of our days by putting on our breath.
4. Come, Brothers, Sisters, sing for joy! The Gift of God made
known is wrapped in tissue and in trim as mortal as our own.

Mr. Watts and the Whirlwind
Andre Watts Recital, TCU

On Cantey Street a visitor came by
doing a dervish dance in the parking lot.
But we didn't know. We were listening
to Mr. Watts play the *Appassionata*.
(I almost thought it was old Ludwig
softly applauding, but it was thunder,
faint as the sirens, off-stage.)
Beethoven would have approved, though.
The hands that delicately touched
Scarlatti now smote the stays
and timbers of the Steinway
until it moaned with joy.

We had known, of course, there was danger.
Before Mr. Watts came from the wings
a third time, a messenger appeared:
"A tornado has touched down not far—
it must be determined whether
we ought to proceed to the basement."
But we were safe; and Mr. Watts began.

At intermission we learned more—
The twister really had come by, and we
all left to see the destruction.
Autos on top one another or shoved aside
as by an impatient hand, canty
off Cantey Street, you might say,
if only a few. It was all random.
Not at all like that perfect storm
Mr. Watts cleanly and powerfully
struck on the keys and strings.

Maybe it heard and was jealous. It was
a fairly minor tornado as winds go,
But we who had ears will remember
how the two touched down all at once,
a finger of terror from the skies,
those hands of unthinkable skill.

⌒

At the Van Cliburn

The exploit is not in the hands hovering
but the stoop, the multiple strike,
   the quick cascade;
more even than that: a mind discovering
deep in its honeycomb a golden store.
I relish that violence made
on my listening drums, or that faint
reluctant, resonant complaint,
a whisper passing in the corridor,
yet one thing most puts me in awe:
the chemistry, whatever bond can be
that ties together finger and brain
in instantaneous prodigy.

How can mind warehouse that rich train,
produce it without fear or flaw
into the astonishment of our ears?
Patterns, nuances I do not guess,
rain from these nerves unstintedly.
Till I ask myself: what skillfulness
in all that of human frame appears
matches this flow, this passionate harmony?

~

A Few Leaves from Lindheimer
The Botanic Research Institute of Texas

Old Lindheimer's hand
plucked off this branch in the Hill Country
over a hundred years ago,
one May, in 1857,
Im wunderschönen Monat Mai,
"when all the flowers were springing."
And here it is, pressed, dried, and mounted
on stiff paperstock, safe these years
in herbariums. Named in Latin,
"Berberis trifoliolata," a bush
for berries you can brew to jelly
once ripening in June. We know it by
the Mexican for "little sour,"
Agrito, Agarita, Algerita,
or say some, "Currant of Texas."
These are more than sharp, spined leaves,
set in a palmate pattern of three,
fastened on paper. They are one leaf
themselves, out of our history.
The man, Lindheimer, who was he?
A refugee from the Fatherland,
a hothead meaning to fight for Texas,
arrived too late at San Jacinto.
A pillar of that colony, New Braunfels,
an editor of strong convictions.
Friend to Comanches, who in awe
watched as he gathered medicine.
A man with a cart and a trained eye,
wandering in hardship and in joy
for a work of love. A score of plants
honor his name—as he does theirs—
instance the one of five yellow petals.
"Lindheimer's Daisy," "Texas Star."

Fixed on stiff paper, in the stacks
of specimen on specimen,
what foresight preserved, how do we value?
It tells of search for understanding
by those who went forth on hill and prairie,
through swamp and stone: it asks for words
and for splendid music: it utters
our thankfulness for things beautiful,
delight in intricacies unveiled,
our hope for powers hidden. Who knows
the chemistries that lie sleeping here,
a brooding knowledge waiting to unfold,
what green enlightenment about to bloom?

Showdown at the Amon Carter

How could they foresee this perfect place
for calling each other out? Those doors,
look at them, ten feet high, of smoky glass,
downtown Cowtown stained on their face?
But here they are: north end, Charlie Russell,
late out of Great Falls, Montana,
sold half his output to pay for whiskey;
in the south corner, Frederic Remington,
a little stiff from the military
but a man, they said, who knew the horse.

If you think to pick which
owns the better hand, check the record.
Both do justice to buffalo, Indian,
flat-topped buttes and rangy crags,
big skies full of stars, arroyos, bears
(especially grizzlies) most of all, horses.
Get down to the small touches:
Charlie takes roots, pine trees with gnarls,
old skulls, rock piles with black cracks,
a deal of unnoticeable detail
(that King of Hearts plain in the dust).
He savvies action, he speaks for Violence.
His horse is no horse unless it's twisted.
Fredric like as not will blur a rock;
he works to paint crisis in the air,
lather a whole skyful in one tone
that threatens to happen. Horses for him
stand like proud women much of the time,
poised, self-confident, aware of their sleekness.

Both of them know their scene is ending;
desperate men, they hold back time
before it wipes out the brave, wild ways.
Count on Russell to let his brush spurt;
he paints shades of blood: the dawn's flush,
squaw skin, gunbursts, wounded flesh,
sandstone hills. He can mold faces
of wax with his hands out of sight
under the table. It must cost him hard
not to shape color, he dotes on it so.

Remington spreads a little flat,
lets pigment slowly swallow your eye—
except those bay horses (he knows every kind
but Lord, he loves bays). Sometimes goes green:
a wash of viridian, maybe,
to bring down biting cold and terror of night
stark on your civilized cheek.
Always he probes for character,
someone come round to the final act
(that Indian sentinel in the snow
at the forest edge in freezing half-light—
what kind of clawed foot floats in the dark?)
Look at that wild, magnificent Dash—
all of those horses like Pegasus flying—
there's organization. He thinks, paints order.

The two of them haven't been long
out of upstairs rooms. Maybe they've taken
too much raw linseed with their drink
and so been goaded into confrontation.
If I have to choose, my man is more likely
Charlie Russell. Only because
I grew up on books by James Willard Schultz:
his Blackfeet Indians and Rocky Mountains,
Ptamakin, Running Eagle, the great snows,
    rock slides.
His country already stretched in my mind
when I found Charlie had laid on color.
A lady in Great Falls, Montana,
sniffed when I told her we had some of his
in Fort Worth. She said Amon bought the lot
of the barkeep's estate. Took off the cream.

So here they're pitted in a hot duel
in the far ends of the first floor.
Any such fracas, it's plain onlookers
are going to get caught in a mean crossfire,
maybe sustain some lasting wounds.
Where is there anyone thinks he can say
which draws the deadlier? the livelier?
Lovers they are, of sagebrush, mountains,

tough men, stage coaches, and again, horses.
Why should a man paint flowers,
fruit baskets, faces, sunsets, seascapes
once he has mastered horses?

Let it come down to a decision
which one dips deeper, closer to heart
or fixes it faster so it will stick—
it's going to end up in a border stand-off.
If it's true there's only one kind of best,
can't it come packaged in different brands?

∾

SOME OF THE PEOPLE

Listening to the Screwdriver

Even with my dull ear I can detect
a grinding somewhere in that crossed complex
of wheels and pulleys. Metal complaining,
saying it won't put up with more neglect.
He listens a moment, and then asks
do I have a long screwdriver? While I go
to find one, I wonder: he wouldn't dare
stick a screwdriver in that whirring maze?
But he does. Gravely, with a physician's
    touch,
he sets the metal tip against a housing,
then bends down and puts his ear
to the wooden handle. Repeats the ritual
at another point. Tells me do the same.
Sure enough, I can hear. Something runs here
smooth as a faucet. But under the
    screwdriver
the alternator curses, grinding away.

Never in all my life I've used a screwdriver
for a stethoscope. Where did he learn this
    art?
Not from me, though this is my son,
who bears the name I bear. For I
with all of a bent toward words and sounds,
know little of motors, of mechanics.
Here's mastery I'm not versed in.
The skill has jumped a generation,
down from another father who could stretch
a web of steel—pull-rods and pumping jacks—
through pine and sassafras on red hills,
taking delight in harnessing power.

All of which tells me, if I'm not obtuse,
there are as many ways to grasp the world
as there are men. More subtleties
of hand, of eye, of ear, imagination,
than imagination itself takes measure of,
than eye or ear can hope to record,
or hand, though it strive, ever set down.

                                 ~

The First Cliff Swallow of April

Over the muddy and diminished river
the first cliff swallow of spring curves upward;
he is looking for some other swallow;
he knows where he is: at this stolid bridge
over the Trinity. A good place, to be sure,
for gathering mud, for affixing a nest
up under the concrete beams. It will be cool,
completely safe against intruders.
The blurt of traffic above can be borne with,
all day, all night. There will be plenty
of gnats and mosquitoes. An adequate place
for a reasonably diligent swallow.

Once in the Thirties I walked down here
when I was a boy, with my father.
He was out of a job, and the bridge
was unfinished. He liked seeing steel
being put to work. All of his life
he lived near steel, shaped it in fire,
quenched it, drilled it. A birth certificate
names my father a "blacksmith."
Not quite exact, but near enough.
We had our look. A few weeks later
oil blossomed in East Texas, he was taken
to live and stretch steel webs, happy again,
but out of my growing and learning days.

A half century flown, the bridge still stands,
and I, here on the same terrain
he brought me to, stay. The swallows go
where? Peru, Argentina, for the winter?
I've lived most of my life in this place,
as much sanctuary as any could ask,
a place to dream of fabulous voyage,
and a port to come back to after flight.

We live wherever a nest can be made.
That father's brood has long since grown,
left the nest. One only of a family
still here in an old neighborhood.
Who brought him here lie long in earth
where he shall lie.

                                      I think of them,

seeing the swallows regain their place
in the groins of the bridge,
reconnoitering, mating, constructing,
founding once more the shape of home.

Lori Swinging

Under the elm next door
Lori swings as she sings;
holding the ropes with her hands,
her head thrown back so far
her beautiful, long red hair
drags in the dust as she swings.

Cowtails and Crabgrass

Back when he worked at the Swift's plant
(in the refrigerator section)
coming out on a hot July evening
he couldn't keep his eyes steady.
He was afraid to go downtown—
the cops would llkely pick him up
for another drunk. It made him wonder
whether the job had giddied his mind.

It was a famous place for squeezing
the last full measure out of everything.
Even the ants leave bones,
but here bones went into fertilizer.
He knew men in the packing house
who collected cow brushes (ends of tails)—
they used them to fill mattresses.
But then (maybe the heat made him think
of it) he knew other people
who did the same with crabgrass.

He got to studying. You can see
why someone would find a use
for all that hair—nobody likes loose ends—
but it took genius to discover
a function for crabgrass. It must
have been a gardener, like him,
who didn't know whether to curse or pray
when the first pale leaves began to slit
brown soil the last of April.
Whoever, he must have had a mission,
a passion for utility in life,
to think of hoeing up the pest
and stuffing it in a mattress.
A kind of vengeance, being able
to sleep on the dry bodies of a weed,
getting to hear it groan a little
ever you turn to a fonder dream?

A Single Trumpet at the Gate

Arriving like that in the blade-thin nick
of time is no good, it won't do.
We know it doesn't convince. Too slick
for a modern taste, the plot shows through.

Yet I remember when you were boys
we listened to *Lenore* while we ate:
when all built to that preposterous noise
of the trumpet's triumph at the gate.

How we all stopped with lifted spoons
halfway to mouths while the clear cascade
of treble fell in cold festoons.
More than our ears, our blood was swayed.

Save my head's hold on that high pitch,
that harbinger trumpet, crisp fanfare.
You. Wherever. Keep your minds rich.
Think how we listened, spoons in mid-air.

A Rock of the Alleghenies

I remember him among forges,
the snarl of flames, the crunch of the bull press,
folding pink steel. Alive in pine woods,
emperor among pumping jacks.
The sound of him, eating an apple
with quick bites; cracking a mittened hand
with a fast ball, intoning ancient verses.
I think I liked him best
singing those earthy Irish ditties
learned in the Allegheny h;ills.

I can remember sleeping on his thigh
in church, and how he followed Bernard McFadden
Ed "Strangler" Lewis, strong men everywhere.
Couldn't he turn up a full-length sledge
with one fist at the handle-end? He was always
making outlandish love (my mother protesting
but loving back). I threw away the bat
he gave me—he called it a "pump handle"—
I wanted to forget the place I flung it
but couldn't when he told me that was what
real players called it. He had crooked thumbs
foul tips in Holyoke, Terre Haute, and Tulsa
made authentic.

He was cheated once,
more times disappointed than we guessed.
And thinking he could kill infection
by working up a sweat, he died too early.
I used to see him every day in sons,
and lately in granddaughters catch him still.
They do not know the words but the Scotch-Irish lilt
and the wild tenderness rise. Sometimes my own bones
brew up a tempest in them, and the throat
wants to let go mad syllables of delight.

$\sim$

Farewell to the Commodore
Basil Muse Hatfield

What we have here is another launching,
not much of a waterway and no vessel
to send on its way to the sea.

All we have is a canful of ashes
kept these forty-five years on a shelf
and these who come to do honor

(or out of a curious itch
to see how the crumbs whirl
when dumped from the side of a bridge).

It's a hot August day. A brisk wind
is stirring the pecan tree boughs
under which we gather for shade.

You can see the bloodweed by the bank
is moving; even the Trinity River
backs up as the south wind pushes.

Under the bridge, tucked up in the ribs,
we notice mud nests of cliff swallows
(they aren't around for the funeral).

The fiddlers, though, are here in good number.
Just as the Commodore asked—
he wanted no sad music.

The speakers are here, and the TV crew
to record a moment in history.
A white fire engine stands by

in case of heatstroke or collapse.
There's even a stout, bewhiskered fellow
who looks like the Commodore's clone.

After the speeches the family climbs
above, to one side of the bridge.
We walk to the river edge to watch

the first sprinkle of powder being cast.
It is caught by the breeze and wafted north;
hardly a grain ever reaches water.

Then a mass of ashes spills downward.
These are the mortal remains, remember,
of a man who made his way by scow

down the Trinity River, the Coastal Canal,
all the way up the Mississippi
on to the Chicago World's Fair. No small feat,

done for his dream of a barge canal
carved out of an insignificant stream
linking our inland town to the Gulf.

Basil Muse Hatfield, called Commodore,
disappeared with his vision some forty years
past. The Trinity still flows unvexed,

and his dust spreads forth in a little cloud,
silently breaches the silent waters,
once more sets out for a distant sea.

⁓

Mr. Harold Taft

Mr. Harold Taft, a gentleman of graphics and gauges,
does not live by the map on which he has carefully
      plotted
the current weather offensive. Nor even by that
      clockwise-circling
Cyclopean eye in its fine frenzy rolling,
which seeks out oncoming barrages. Nor even by
his bones, attuned as they are to the encroaching
of seasons and odd circumstance. Modest
and cheerful as he is, having been schooled in
      humility
on a grandiose scale (his subject violently objects
to analysis, only reluctantly yields
piecemeal particulars), he lives
by accumulating data, much as they say
a raindrop is saved up, accomplished, a bit
of moisture here, a piece of vapor there
until a respectable concentration has been
      gathered.
He has a touch of the uncanny in him:
reading the rhythms of the air, taking
      temperatures
much like a wife who tests her fertility,
he dares to say whether the welkin
will bring forth. His is a fatherly concern,
peering out anxiously into the void
to say whether ominous red patches have that
      hook
by which folks are caught in tumultuous turns.

Mr. Harold Taft has, of course,
a love affair with the elements,
wishes it to be understood, notwithstanding,
that no matter how accurately he foretells
or for that matter how badly he misses,
he is not responsible for whatever happens.
or for that matter, how badly he misses,
No, strictly speaking, his is a calculation
of ambiguous factors at work on partially-known
      quanta,
not immutable law though very good likelihood.

No one, so far as is known, has ever ascribed
        calamity
to an Act of Harold Taft. This enables him
to remain cheerful, happy among charts and dials
and the partly predictable perchance of weather.

Nor let it be said the fact is forgotten:
Mr. Taft also plays, for our delectation,
a wind instrument. ⁓

Seneca Xenophon Swimme

Remembering, how can I stay a smile?
For his name alone sings. Think of it:
Seneca Xenophon Swimme. How can I help,
for a glorious classical name like that—
(look how the Roman and Greek entwine)....
A great tall man, with a large bald head.
I saw him once at a tent revival,
sitting up front, hat on his head,
and I thought, the fellow has poor piety.
Later I learned—he was an elder
in the Methodist church. And he kept his hat on
because his head was cold.
                              But once again,
that incredible name! Who was his father,
his mother, to set that grandiose name?

I met him in a newspaper shop
where I hoped to learn the trade of reporter.
He was using the Linotype to print
his book, *A Composite Gospel,*
all four of them, and no event missing.
I invited him to have dinner with us,
and he told us some of his life.
How he had married a mountain girl
back East somewhere, I suppose.
She couldn't read, so he taught her—
reading, for one thing, who but Shakespeare?
From one thing he told he had a sharp eye:
that Mary (my wife) was one of two
of the prettiest girls in all Riverside
(I've always thought she was The One).
I looked in the library to find his name
in a Methodist book but had no luck.

So I'll never know how, why, that name
makes history shout. And I'm envious.
There are William's, of course, in literature:
Shakespeare, Wordsworth, Bryant, and Yeats—
I'll never add mine to a list like that.
though Barney's a sound enough name, I think,
it doesn't quite ring like the name "Swimme,"
with "Seneca Xenophon" spreading their wings. ~

A Grass in the Sun

The dwindling year lifts up
beardgrass, bright locks aflare with sun,
marking, for any who think to question,
how folded seed is not daunted
nor root outrun.

What shall I say of her, grass-comely,
her head's corona of soft light—
proof to an earth aslant toward winter
warmth that outshines the approaching cold,
the encroaching night?

Say to those in the fallow darkness
in soil of the yet-to-be-upturned:
she was the fairest of all grasses.
I looked on her when sunlight touched her
and dry straw burned.

~

The Power

After one visit when I brought her dinner,
I saw her true need was to talk:
not vainly as the heathen do (she'd have said)
or randomly like walruses;
no, but for sheer venture, soul-exploring,
for strategies of bliss, for shunning sin,
for sowing chaff and reaping talent.
God gave her once a lovely voice
(she remembered) and then another day
He struck her with the Power of Healing,
so fierce it canceled out all music.

Almost a physical blow when it came,
that Power. God, did I know, seeks out
    His chosen?
Did I recall how Eleazar went
to find a bride for Isaac? The tale typifies
God seeking out a bride (the Church)
for His Son. She liked the word: the Bible's
    full
of typifyings. She'd taught a class once
in a Sunday School nearby. Her text,
that bridal theme—the Song of Solomon—
hard to explain to young Chicanos,
but she liked things not too clear, for
    searching.

Did I believe in laying on of hands?
I must, for she perceived in me
the same gift God might use. In her, though
it diminished, no, it disappeared.
These things happen: what is given, goes.
(I saw she wished for a healing touch—
not the old way of man with woman,
but speech and warmth of human presence,
for she lived all alone in a still house).
At 94, she knew the Power had departed.
The flesh must dispossess itself.
Once she could sing most beautifully
but God had used the voice as bait
to lure her into Healing. Music can soothe

for a moment. It will not cure
a lifelong ache. Touch can, given Power,
as she had been, for working cures,
defeating pain.
                    Strange, though:
at 94 she suffered with her stomach.
A malady no one could find the cause for—
physicians stammered when they diagnosed.
She knew what the matter was:
Power burns out all insulation.

We came on her a fortnight later
perched on a seat in Leonard's Subway,
munching a great sack of popcorn,
gleeful as any schoolgirl playing hookey.
She wasn't going anywhere (she owned)
just back and forth from the parking lot
up through the tunnel under the bluff
into the bowels of the great store
and return. Why not? It was free.
Her name in obituaries I've not seen.
It's possible, she may be riding still
between the stops of whatever's hereafter.
Or maybe by now she's found solace
in pilgrimage, she doesn't intend
to leave our scene until she pleases,
since once she knew—indisputably—Power,
held it herself in her own two hands
till everything between went glowing.
                                        ⌣

There on the Third Page

After all, it was true (she said)
her picture, there on the third page.
Not really important, of course,
she knew that. But anyone who read
couldn't help seeing it was her
(Even if it didn't really show
her exactly right. The photographer

was in a hurry. You know how it is.)
Still, many of her friends knew who
it was. A lot of them cut it out
and mailed it to her. Wouldn't you think
they'd all, every one, be proud she'd got
all that publicity and such? Well,
Phreena, her dearest friend, was not.

She wouldn't even talk about it.
She missed that paper somehow, else
the picture hadn't caught her eye.
Everybody knows it when she tells
one of her whiteys. It was there,
right by the day's obituaries—
the first thing with her breakfast fare.

It touched her mind, with all those copies,
to mail Phreena one just for spite.
Well, not spite, which isn't Christian,
but it would nicely set things right.
She'd wait a day or two, bye the bye,
ask her dear friend had she seen it yet?
It would be 'greevious' to watch her lie. ∼

The Storm

When she stormed out the door, all out-of-doors
itself was brewing up a weather. The night
criss-crossed itself with gnarls of light,
off in the western sky a smothered fire
shuddered but never would die down to dark.
If she stayed out she might be sorry.
She didn't care. It eased her just to walk
and walk she did, up and down the street.
The neighbors might well look out and gawk—
why would a virtuous woman prowl like this?
Even if she wasn't totally discreet,
she wasn't one to traipse for a lark.
The more she thought of her fix, the higher
the flames in her grew. But think she must.
She had to know: had matters come at last
to where she'd have to—
                    What was that?
Thunder. The first, but it was coming. Fast?
She'd have to take the Step. The final one,
how do you do a thing so quick, so flat?

And now a neighbor did come out. "What's wrong?
Is something wrong?" *Of course something is wrong,*
she thought. *Would I be walking like a fool
out in the weather?* But all she said was "Yes."
I've got to decide if I'll ever go back
inside that house. And she turned to her walking
while her neighbor stood in blank dismay.

A little stray gust came soft and cool.
It was just as well. Having had to say
what her trouble was rearranged her mind.
It must have decided the weather, too,
for the flashing began to wither away,
the thunder forgot what it had been stalking,
the western sky began to blind,
the night grew quiet and comfortably black.

Was it a sign? Not probably, she thought.
But I'll go back in, once more, like as not.
                                    ⌒

The Wedding

She woke cloudily at five; rose; came quickly
to her kitchen before the sun made morning.
Bees already would be searching, and out of her
      head
more honey-gatherers went abroad.
He was not in his accustomed chair. The young
      man.
She would have gladly brought him a hot cup,
whatever he might choose for victual.
She listened: but there was no noise above
in the room. She wondered much about him.
She wondered much about herself.
He came, he went, according to his will,
spoke very little, yet his voice was warm.
She could not tell what thoughts moved him,
if indeed any moved. Still, his eye
seemed friendly.
           There were parks, of course,
banks by the river to promenade—
he might have asked her company
but he did not. Somewhere between aloof and
      shy,
was that how she would count him?
She gathered up the dishes, washed them,
sorted them carefully as well her thoughts.

At ten mid-morning a friend came,
curious, excited by the startling news.
Why hadn't she told—downright deceitful—
to be married this day and telling no one!
Of course it was true. The notice posted
down at the court house, everything arranged,
no doubt to keep hidden from her friends.
She blushed, protested, was not believed.

Whatever nonsense was this? Her heart loped
faster than it had any business to.
After a while she closed the place,
walked the two blocks in a cold haste,
climbed the solid granite steps.
It said what it said. She dried her forehead
and retraced her way. What ought she do
about this impertinence? At 2 p.m.
she'd scarcely have lunch dishes done,
put away. And now she must
see to the meal. She had no time
to think about it—how could one think
of such a thing even given time?
She found herself laughing at the absurdness
even while serving customers. They looked
at her, wondered at her queer behavior.

At 1:30 all were gone. She stared
into a mirror but the person there
offered no counsel. Almost
mechanically she studied her closet,
selected a dress and put it on.
It wasn't, she thought, the best she had
but it was blue. Once he had said
he liked blue. She wanted very much
to please him when he came at 2:00
with the minister. Blue. He'd be pleased.

∼

The Touch

At fourteen her fingers had already learned
what they would still be doing at fourscore:
playing an out-of-tune piano in a church.
Time was her fingers moved more blithely;
long-using took from what had been before.

Around their noon of life he took his notion:
it would be well she mastered other keys.
No telling how it might be provident—
she could shift for herself with market skills
once he was gone. The world pays arts like these.

Once he was gone. She knew it wasn't so.
That bond being broken, what would be left
for her to do on an earth rattling loose?
And those much-labored fingers, how could she
admonish them to flutter and be deft?

But she obediently began. At the machine
we watched her patiently sit and peck away.
And children that we were, we tittered. For
no matter how persistently she strove
it mostly read f f f j j j.

Her fingers must have wondered why they plucked
so stiffly, like a military band,
when there were hymns they knew and could be playing.
While hope stilled whispered in her singing ear,
they knew all other ground was sinking sand.

She never learned the touch. And he was gone
before they knew the harvest wouldn't reap.
And we, when we remember how we laughed
in secret at that grave staccato beat
laugh still, a little. So as not to weep.

Tincey

On the way down to Frenchman Street
F. asked, suddenly, I let him stop
at a two-story house. He went up
and spoke; a fellow small and neat
answered the door. "Mr. Eggleston,
you haven't paid your rent," F. began.

(I saw right away who it was
he spoke to—it was Tincey;
the big house was haven for his fancy
ladies. You didn't give his kind a cause
for trouble. He'd a mean reputation,
enough to teach a bold man caution.)

"Oh," said Tincey. "Sorry about that."
And he pulled out a wad of bills,
extracting from it appropriate peels.
Mere money was no object, not
to Tincey. He could harvest more
if mishap laid his cupboard bare.

F. wasn't happy, staring in the house;
a look of loathing crossed his face.
"Your dogs are chewing up the place!"
Did it bother Tincey Eggleston?
"How much?" he asked, lifting his wad.
In no time F. was satisfied.

Out at the curb I lived to tell
this tale. And F. lived to old age.
Tincey, he kept a winning edge
until one day they found him in a well.
The house came down, the ladies made
     a switch;
on high ground arose a mighty church.

⁓

(The "I" is not "I", but a fellow-worker,
J. D. Davis, who told me this story.)

THE TOWN

Selected Views of the Court House

Almost a century that imposing pile
of freckled granite, bare to the sun,
has lifted a dome on the high bluff
where the founders camped. Even today
it enters the circle of the present:
passing by on a Sunday morning, suddenly
I see for the first time
a shadow dulling the great stone:
between it and the sun a tower rises,
casts a soft image of itself
north through the town, over
the copper cupola.

        It is never too late
to change (the shadow says). History is old.
That granite, once a molten seep,
is eons older. And shadow came to be
when the first light went on.

            Another day,
passing alongside, I look in surprise
into the glass of other windows,
and, shimmering there in the liquid bronze,
the ancient court house floats, like a bride
adorned for the aisle, a ship
quivering toward champagne.

            The world is new;
change, that fastidious brush,
dips into numberless pigments.
Everything that has been becomes
and now is, and even while we look,
dissolves, resolves into other faces,
water of time, shattering as it moves.
          ~

Traffic Pattern

Over the bluff where the troopers camped,
where (they say) lean men on horseback
drove their herds down to the river;
over the solid court house, hard in its hundred years
of granite, little blue herons rise in flight.
They move from the heronry near the river,
bivouac of egrets and herons in a grove.
It is nothing to them, acids and power
occupy men; they have their ancient tasks
of breeding, nesting, forays into fields.
Immature little blues, wholly white
in their plumage, take wing; the cattle egrets too
ride the updrafts along the sheer bluff,
loft the tall dome, and head through the pass
of the two great pylons, the latest growth
sheathed in their shining.

                  Birds and towers are new;
the heronry two, three years. The cattle egrets
inched north only yesterday out of Brazil.
We hardly saw how the mix was made:
here where the bawling cattle clouded streets,
where the frontier post slowly became
a village, a town, a coruscant city
lifting its glass and gleaming stone
into a traffic pattern for flashing wings,
acceptance, accommodation arrive.

The currents of change circle about;
they spin old perspectives like dead leaves.
How do we measure what our place will be?
No man knows the future; by what divination
can he name the wings, the plodding feet,
the faces of inhabitants to come?
Roughly we shape a pattern
out of a pattern that has given shape.
The feet, the wings, the faces, they will come.

                                   ~

A Rose in Winter

We always can tell when it comes;
there where the two forks of the river join
below the bluff, a great white billow
rises.

Floating storms of condensing steam,
escape from the power plant.
Winter puts on one of its softer
guises.

Petals of vapor puffed up at the edge
of our town, a smoke that says
somewhere a raging fire must be
consuming.

But all I can think of in the swirl
is an old haunting, slow chorale
in a Chrismas key: *Lo, How a Rose
E'er blooming.*

A Modern Stonehenge

Men think to trap the sun
because in its annual trek
it always circles back
to the place where the year's begun—
to hang at a measurable height
cross-haired in a sextant sight.

Except for seeing it sink,
a red bullseye going down
between smokestacks in our town,
I know no cromlech chink
in which to watch the year
return, exactly in gear.

Looking across the bottom
and up to our western gate
I see those megaliths wait
a given week in our autumn
for the sun dropping down at six
to fire skyscraper wicks

till the city's whole north glass
bursts into dazzling display—
plainly, to prove the day
has come round, come to pass,
come in like the unaging tide
for Time to be certified.

~

The Drovers
Riverside Park, Riverside

Over this bank and bottomland
the strung-out trail herd moved and bawled;
in my mind's hollow I can hear
the mournful noise where they complained:
a music dark, part rage, part fear;
body to lumbering body called.

Here on dry grass I drive
the killdeer, clamorous where I walk;
those birds, an outcry for their name
arise before I ever arrive
at their feeding place; I make a game
chasing the screaming, brittle flock.

The flickers rise up too, but they
and the meadowlark shun protest;
or if they must, it is no such shriek
of indignant pride, to say
like the killdeer with outstretched beak:
this table welcomes no other guest.

Hearing those herds in their rich uproar
old drovers got great pleasure (they said),
braver than men with woods and brass
or a heavenly chorus they swore.
And I, chousing killdeer over the grass,
taste a raw harmony in my head.

More than cattle and birds are driven
(so thinks the drover, pursuing wings);
there is a listener with cool ear
struck with the antics of a breed given
to uproar. Who leans close to hear
the resonance of their quaverings?

Imploded
Medical Arts Building

Nothing in Nature dies like this:
a redwood toppled swings an arc
full ninety degrees and stretches
its ruin out. A coarse-stemmed gourd
gnawed by the borer wilts away,
collapses into a yellow shrivel.
Glaciers let go huge lump by lump,
great dribbles of themselves into sea.
This artifact of air, glass, stone,
its roots being pulverized
in an instant, almost dreamily
quivers and begins to faint,
to wrinkle in upon itself
into a pitiable mound of rubble.

Do men and women meet downfall
so? Slain men on battlefields—
that Spanish soldier, caught in mid-death,
the bullet spurting into his head;
some ballerina turned a swan,
neatly depositing her flesh
into a huddled remnant; a child
fantasizing an old fable,
a mimic to catastrophe?

How fitting here, this thing of stone
and glass and air, made by Man's hand,
should fail like him—strength sapped away,
alien element storming in
from all sides, earth with ineluctable pull
reaching, and all coming down, coming slowly
down, with a sort of puzzled look,
knowing it was not made to last
but not having thought at all of this,
to be so suddenly dust and bones.

The Lions Shall Eat Straw
The Flatiron Building

The high gagged lions
staring in stone from cornices
sullen, aloft,
have in each blunt, carnivorous jaw
straw.

Whoever carved
those horrendous gapes of snarling teeth
to scare the street
had little thought of the dull weak
beak

that scours the alleys
and plucks up scrap to shape a nest.
The glazed eyes set
fixedly, disdain to taste that profane
stain.

The stone fangs bare,
helpless to mince or down this meat—
O Lions, Lords—
roar, scatter the verminous rash
trash!

⁓

The Ruins

Like a ruined abbey
or a bombed cathedral,
the broken walls loom up over the yards
where the cattle, the swine came.
The roofless rooms look out
absent of any purpose.
The red bricks age slowly.
Weeds infest foundations.

Here they have stood for years
after the gutting fires,
of cork-lined rooms burning for weeks;
they never could incinerate
these vast cubes of sullen stuff
too savagely strong today
to warrant demolition—
Are they left as a remembrance
of vanished trade, a thriving time?
when animals by thousands,
a torrent of flesh, passed through?

The tread, the moans, are stilled,
only a name remains to say
here was a charnel house.
We know the product now
only in commercial display,
but here the deed was done
turning live beast into food.

You'd think the city would compel
someone to tear these ruins down.
Better, maybe, they still stand
as ruined sentinels of the past,
a raw reminder of old days
when a city was shaped, a history
made in mortar and red meat.

~

A Bullsnake under Belknap Bridge

The bullsnake under the bridge where we went
    looking for swallows,
he had reason to lie there, half of his hide
    extended,
half of him plunged in a hole (did it keep
    his bowels cool,
stashing his tail-end in the dirt?) When he
    saw us, though, how splendid
the way he rejected our presence! If only
    he'd had hands
to have thumbed his nose—the way he slowly
    withdrew,
no sound of reversing gears, nothing of any
    struggle;
disengaging his notice from whatever he'd
    meant to do,
he effortlessly slid himself down like a
    rubber band
coming back to itself. How beautiful!
    How elastic!
And we stood watching, pleased that anything
    could go smoothly.

That a snake can go forward is, when uou think,
    fantastic:
without any legs it proceeds in a cursive
    geometry
from A to B, not too squarely, not exactly
    Euclidean—
but to back down a hole without being sucked
    like sphagetti!
The nonchalance of it, the art, so utterly
    ophidian.

       ~

A Paean for Prionopsis

The high yellow flowerheads rise
in August air
six feet, teetering upon green poles
completely unaware
the age of blooming long since passed;
drouth and hot sun possess the land.

Each with a juggler's art
sits tipsy on a wand
oblivious it performs a feat
like those skyscrapers beyond
there on the bluff in hazy sight
stretched skinnily into sky.

Old Prionopsis
of the sawtooth leaves,
I much admire your upright stance,
your standing golden in loose sheaves,
your garish tops, giddy in the summer wind,
like shuttlecocks in warm butter dipped.

Thomas Nuttall, that original eye,
first gave you habitation and a name
for us to know you by.
But where's an acknowledgment of your right
to honor for fresh finery?

Those who have borne
the heat of this land—
they have always known it is possible:
life can withstand
even surmount the unendurable,
draw from the glazing kiln form burned beautiful.

~

(*Prionopsis ciliata*, the sawtooth daisy, of the Trinity River bottoms)

Singing in Mulberry May

Singing in Mulberry May that resonant thrush
        knows such liquidity, I think
he hides in a rain-barrel echo-chamber,
        articulating sweet funk
in soft ascending passages a slow mind strains
        to gather.

        I have wished a long time to say
the Swainson makes the month memorable by his
        fluted simple, repeated tattoo,
which, what it lacks in bravura and passion,
        it more than makes up to the ear
by its candor, its delicate understatement
        of much the mind need not bear. ❧

The Ginkgoes at the Water Garden

The ginkgoes at the Water Garden
spread their green fans like Chinese gentlemen
a genial company of clones.
They stand in a courtly listening-to,
thinking, perhaps, of Po-Chu-i, Li Po,
and the clink of oars, lute music offshore.
Much more there is of an ancient past
gathered about these tiers of stone
whose waters suck down history
than some queer future here unswallowed.

Sadly, maiden fruits are fetid;
the gentlemen, therefore, have no ladies.
The fastidious single ginkgo himself,
famous for disdaining pollution,
tough city dweller, how does he manage,
no romance in life, to keep chlorophylling?

Not only are they strangers in this land,
they are not of this epoch;
always they hear the mountain streams,
the howling monkeys, the rustling bamboo
muffling the traffic's grind. They stand
in a surround of geometrical space,
of indeterminate time, impassive,
aloof, imperturbable,
survivors, no matter what may come.

~

A Park by the Trinity River
Riverside Park

Bending like this enables the bones:
my pockets bulge in filling up
with a round hoard of sleek pecans—
cast down so thick for a gleaner to find
in a five-nut or a six-nut stoop—
more for a quick, commodious hand.

It sharpens the eye to pick them out
of fallen leaves and bottom soil;
mine wants to give a triumphant shout
whenever it spots the splitting hull
or the rich nugget of brindled brown
out of the husk, naked, undone.

Days now they've fallen, a slow rain—
more like a sift of meteorites.
Stooping, I hear one plummet down
to tell me there are more to come,
give the great trees their frosty nights
and the norther pulling a ragged comb.

Never before have I had my fill
of such a crop. Nobody will starve
because at home I've a heaped-up pail—
not one nut more than I deserve.
They were here for the taking and I took.
Let someone prove it miserlike.

Our fathers sawed off branches whole
and men still beat the patient boughs.
Even I fill my pockets till
they swell like gopher-cheeks stuffed full.
Now, as I climb up Dalford Hill
the plump nuts trail me to my house.

~

Once the Ear Wakes to Listen

Once the ear wakes to listen, night
fills with a thousand sayings:
the grumbling tom-tom of the diesel
growling rail yards; the calculated crash
of freight cars; whine and wheel of gears
of semi's pushing through the city;
three kinds of siren in their unique screaming
moving from near to far and disappearing;
a mockingbird ecstatically mad
in the drench of moonlight; the bubbling flute
of a screech owl in the midnight dark;
somewhere a baby crying; unintelligible voices;
a jet faint as a buzzing fly overhead;
cars passing on the street, for unknown reasons;
the creak of ties on a railroad bridge
and the horn of the Amtrak; dogs,
always dogs, practicing anger;
cats in their agony of sex;
stairs creaking, adjusting their wooden teeth;
a wind chime like ice clinking;
a fan exhaling, a radio thumping.
Her soft breath on the pillow;
this too a solemn cadence, almost undetectable,
somewhere in the bedding, a heart beating.

⁓

Westward Lightning

flutters like a rapt cellist's searching fingers
sure of string yet wavering, subtly pressing,
half in passion to shut off, and partly throttling
with one hand what the other summons; like a
mare's flank twitching under the fly, westward
lightning flinches the night. Some shuttered mirror
signaling, a guttering in far darkness
of blown candles in deep caverns, the fire flickers
violently and without earthly purpose
other than splitting space and spelling out how
force knows bounds where greater force is futile.
All that shuddering when the terror rises,
when cold cloud and kindling strain toward inward
fusion—how can the white-hot mantle falter,
quench in blackness the bright spasm, how when
outer can never stifle inner tumult,
form more than an instant master content,
flashing cancel, calm that turbulent tinder?

Twelve Inches of Snow

Unrelentingly it sifts down,
accumulates: it stifles the bared land
and a great stillness comes about
as if a cold Vesuvius burst
its dead caldera and is casting out
upon our world.

We are a new Pompeii, a Herculaneum;
now in the streets the chariots
no longer rattle; the bridges bar
all travel. Even the rails are silent
and overhead no roar. The market place
is vacant, the forum noiseless. The famous signs,
the Caveat Canem, the obscene paintings,
the ordinary words of ordinary lives
all are obliterated.
Somewhere perhaps a sentinel,
as in the *Book of Knowledge* of my boyhood
watches the end approach, holds to his post.

Are we brothers to those fossil insects
trapped in the shale at Florissant?
Sealed in our day by volcanic fury?
Time, that slippery stuff,
piles over and between our breathing.
The life we thought we knew ceases to be.

〜

The Crones
B52s, Carswell AFB

Like bent old women shuffling off to bed,
the great gray planes go clambering the stair
upward to flight; they clutch at wind and air
and mumble in the dark of a grim dread.
Between unpitying sphere and the black spread
of starless sky, a creaking hallway where
the sterile moon holds up its shrunken flare
to light their stark way, they clumsily tread.

Yet once aloft, they lean with hoyden grace
into the jetstreams that carouse the height;
they run like pagans in an attic chase,
bacchants that rouse the town in wild dellght.
They pierce with shrill hilarity cold space
and shake the solemn temple of the night.

$\sim$

Sugarberries and Kneebones

September. Walking down Dalford Hill,
I pick from the sugarberry tree—
those pea-sized fruits a shade past orange,
little red apples of delicacy.

Hardly the bait to dispossess Adam,
not much but peel on a hard seed within;
I nip through sweet pulp and stolidly think:
where did I meet with so tender a skin?

Where, where, in all of a swarming city
(the humility of it makes me proud)
does the taste of the sugarberry drool
through a happier cheek, a richer-endowed?

And now I remember where I came
on leather flimsy as this clasping these—
down in a closet where I searched
in the dark on my hands and my skinny knees.

What I found there was a painful fact:
the pads that cover my bending bones
have withered, there isn't left as much
as the moss on a couple of old tombstones.

A Birthdayful of Beard-Tongues
Oakhurst: Scenic Drive

The beard-tongues rise out of the limestone bluff
just as they did a half-century ago
when I was a boy wandering on these hills.
The seams of crumbling rock, the calcareous soil
have not changed. Soft rains and warming sun of April
unlock their chemistries and a swarm of flowers
covers the slope, this year in profusion.

I do not remember the passing of years.
Who that is part of the sea recalls every wave?
They arrived, surged through, moved on
much as that ancient ocean did, laying down
this chalk. I too entered this world one April
and have been ever since a disciple of green.
Only the calendar tells me on this day
I am sixty-five, and the histories say
not many times more will I find these towers
lifting their tinted bells. No difference
to them nor probably to me if they
still celebrate a good time to be born,
to spring up from the fertile earth
and silently peal the change of season.
They will not toll for any: their own delight
is their mission. Nor need they. Not far off
he will not hear, who saying his nunc dimittis,
took part of this richness where he went.

An Edge of Light

The city hangs now like a golden cage
within December's cave, a feast of light
wrought in the fervid mind of some cold mage
who dreams a hearth to mitigate the night.

Men coming from the East may see it glow—
no blazing brand, no topaz of the rich,
but lamplight plainer folk might think to show,
a halo warm against the western pitch.

Earth boasts wide cities that bedazzle more,
which, come upon from air at sundown, shine
magnificently, with a burning core;
they make our hill a village in design.

Maybe the limestone bluff, that horseshoe bend
of river, bound together make a moat,
distance enough to haze a garish trend,
rampart enough to dull the modern note.

Elsewhere great towers into night retreat;
look how a skyline, rimmed in kerosene,
is lifting up an edge of light to meet
the dark: our town will have its time of sheen.

Oak Leaves Blowing at Mount Olivet

In the encampment for the dead
the downed leaves will not be still;
while we are gathered to remember,
while obsequies are said,
maddened by the south wind
the leaves hurl themselves unceasingly
over the withered grass
beneath the stiff post oaks.
Their motion seizes my eye,
till I ask of their wheel and shuffle,
where have I seen you before?

Contours of surf I've seen come sliding in,
boiling, no sooner the one beached
than another, riding its back,
follows. Blackbirds I've watched
settle upon a field, reeling,
leapfrogging, the hindmost
tumbling across the van.
In old movies I remember
hordes of driven bodies
swarming in a wild charge,
giving no thought to the fallen.
I have stared at sleek machines
spurting one sheet atop another.
But never so frenzied a tumult
as this, lifting up, casting forward,
seething, this mindless movement,
this overthrow of the leaves.

Here in this quiet space
where I too one day will lie,
is it fitting these brittle shapes,
dismantled beyond repair,
cavort in hectic stampede,
taking no notice of us,

our sorrow, our solemnity?
They fall as the season demands,
they do as December bids.

The body shall not be offended,
if, once it returns to soil,
this haste of the leaves should happen.
It would be music to my ears
could they hear. Delight to my eyes,
given vision. And neither being so,
it yet would be well with a kinsman
to both leaf and wind, to the stir
among things of earth, to their dance
before elemental powers, to loss
and acceptance of loss, to at last
a subduing, the still descent into peace.

Acknowledgments

THE LADY AND THE CALLIOPE, *Borderlands*, Austin Texas.

THE CLYDESDALES, *Creative Writing Publication*,
TCU English Department, Fort Worth, Texas.

A WINE VESSEL AT THE KIMBELL, *Creative Writing Publication*,
TCU English Department, Fort Worth, Texas.

THE SLIDE, *New Tex 94*, NTC Press, Denton, Texas.

CANTICLE FOR A CUTTING HORSE, *Permitted Proof*, Kaleidograph Press,
Dallas, Texas; *Southwest Writers Anthology*, Steck-Vaughn,
Austin, Texas; *The Killdeer Crying*, Prickly Pear Press,
Fort Worth, Texas.

A BALANCED WHEEL, *Washing the Cow's Skull, The Killdeer Crying*,
Prickly Pear Press, Fort Worth, Texas.

A MAGNIFICANCE OF MELISMAS, *A Texas Christmas*,
Pressworks Publishing Co., Dallas, Texas.

A CAROL OF THE GIFT OF GOD, *Texas and Christmas*,
TCU Press, Fort Worth, Texas.

A BULLSNAKE UNDER BELKNAP BRIDGE, *Borderlands*, Austin, Texas.

A FEW LEAVES FROM LINDHEIMER, *Riversedge*, UTPA Press,
Edinburg Texas.

A PARK BY THE TRINITY RIVER, Thorp Spring Press, Austin, Texas;
Fort Worth Star-Telegram, October 18, 1981

A SINGLE TRUMPET AT THE GATE, *The Lyric*.

A ROCK OF THE ALLEGHENIES, *Inheritance of light*,
University of North Texas Press, Denton, Texas

FAREWELL TO THE COMMODORE, *Creative Writing Publication*,
TCU English Department, Fort Worth, Texas.

THE DROVERS, *Texas Review*, English Department,
Sam Houston University, Huntsville, Texas.

A PAEAN FOR PRIONOPSIS, *Creative Writing Publication*,
TCU English Department, Fort Worth Texas.

A MODERN STONEHENGE, *A Galaxy of Verse*, Fort Worth Texas.

A BIRTHDAYFUL OF BEARD-TONGUES, *Behold Texas*,
Nortex Press, Austin Texas.

AN EDGE OF LIGHT, *Christmas in Texas*, Brown Rabbit Press,
Houston Texas.

~

About the Author

William D. Barney, a former president of the Poetry Society of Texas and award-winning poet, has lived in Fort Worth since 1928. By the late 1950s, Barney had become a much needed new voice in Texas, attaining national as well as regional recognition. In 1962, William Barney received the Robert Frost Memorial Award from Frost himself. This honor is one of five major awards from the Poetry Society of America. Barney's collections have also won the Borestone Mountain Award, the Kaleidograph Book Award, the Nortex Press Award, and two Texas Institute of Letters awards. Perhaps, one can best measure his art in its inclusion in a remarkable variety of anthologies. He appears in *Out Where the West Begins* (1949), *Southwest Heritage* (1950), *Southwest Writers* (1967), *A Part of Space: Ten Texas Writers* (1960), *Washing the Cow's Skull* (1982), *From Hide and Horn* (1985), *New Texas* (1993 and 1995), *Texas in Poetry* (1994), and *Inheritance of Light* (1996), anthologies edited from dissimilar perspectives. His body of book-length work consists of eight collections of verse along with a memoir. The retired postal worker and former Texas Poet Laureate is an active poet, bird watcher, and naturalist.

~